SHAPING SPIRITS

ACKNOWLEDGEMENTS

Earlier versions of 'No.12 Chalk Grove', 'Family Prayers,' 'Advanced Classics (i) Translation' and 'Advanced Classics (ii) Greek prose with Miss Genochio' have appeared in *The Literary Imagination*; 'Illuminations' and 'Prize Book' in *PN Review*, and 'White on black, black on white', 'Winter afternoon' and 'Scholarship candidate' in the TLS. 'Downing College Natural History Museum' was first published in the anthology *Did I Tell You ? 131 Poems for Children in Need*, edited by Nicky Gould and Vicky Wilson (2010), and 'A Winter's Tale' first appeared in the anthology *Canterbury Festival Poet of the Year* (2015).

I am grateful to Emma Tristram for encouragement and constructive criticism of early drafts of these sonnets. I also thank fellow Darwin Writers Patricia Debney, Nancy Gaffield, Nancy Wilson Fulton, Emmi Iteranta, Jeremy Scott and Howard Bowman, together with Sampurna Chatterji, for their thoughtful responses to later drafts.

For my sisters Teresa and Catherine
who will remember it all differently.

CONTENTS

I

NO. 12, CHALK GROVE

In that cold house on the edge of Cambridge
she's reading alone while we two sleep,
toddler Teresa and me, the new-born baby.
Windows shake and rattle in blasts of sleet
but she's deep in Coleridge's poem
'Dejection', hearing how his wind rose higher
wailing through the night like a lost child
screaming loud to make her mother hear.

Our father is in college, miles away,
ordinands aren't allowed to live at home
although he comes to visit us, some days.
As the days lengthen she wheels our pram
through dark-brown gardens ringing with unheard
children at play and cries of nesting birds.

II

AFTER CHURCH, 1953

Two little girls stand in front of Daddy
and Mummy, backed by the leafy creepered side
of Daddy's college after Sunday matins.
Mummy's dark hair is set off by her light
flowered shirt-waister, Daddy in his cassock
which must be hot, holds Teresa in her checked
summer dress, both smiling. One is absent –
our baby sister Catherine who might act
unsuitably in church or even yell.

Cross and bored by the long
service and now this family pose, I turn
my back on Daddy to cast a shadow on
Mummy's sunlit skirt and legs, too young
and wriggly to agree to stand still.

III

FAMILY PRAYERS

Our baby couldn't read, Daddy was out
at work till late, but Mummy, T. and I
would read together, verse and verse about,
the Evening Psalms appointed for the day.
That sounds like a Victorian novel, and yet
those psalms gripped my mind: the man who swears
unto his neighbour and disappointeth him not
went home, so did the Lord whose *ministers*
are flaming fire, terrible as huge
wheels of flame rolling across the sky,

and curses that she wouldn't let us read,
let them fall, let them consume away
like a snail, roared from their silent page
of promises kept by a jealous God.

HARVEST FESTIVAL

The church was in its party dress, sheaves
of golden wheat bowing heavy heads,
orange carrots and pumpkins, crimson-red
and yellow dahlias, brilliant autumn leaves.
'When you see Daddy coming in to lead
the procession, keep quiet,' Mummy warned,
'and don't shout *That's my Daddy!*' I gave a nod
in silence, rather offended that she thought
I might be such a baby.
                                    But when we chant
The golden-tresséd sun, the hornéd moon
'Mid her spangled sisters, and he stands
in his white robe and golden stole in front
of the altar, I kneel proudly down
and whisper *That's my Daddy!* to my hands.

V

SUNDAY SCHOOL

We learned about the coat of divers colours,
the special present Joseph had from Jacob
his father, which enraged the older brothers
into selling Joseph as a slave,
tearing his coat off, ripping it and staining
the many colours by slaughtering a kid,
then taking the blood-stained rags to Jacob, saying
beasts had torn his favourite to bits.

Divers colours must be dangerous
emerald like sea-water shimmering green,
sapphire, indigo, purple amethyst,
stitched with trembling gold and silver gleams
of scattered little fishes darting out
from the shadow of an approaching mouth.

VI

39, DE FREVILLE AVENUE

The home's heart was the kitchen with the wooden
table we ate at, and the grey iron stove
which burned you if you touched it, and glowed
red when Mummy put in coal. Our garden
had a plum tree, currant bushes, grass.
A weed-grown bit at the end was given to us

for me and Teresa to build our own camp fires,
pick elderberries or climb on to a branch
of the big sycamore beside the wall
to watch our neighbour juggling or riding
his bike with one wheel and no handlebars.
Sometimes he'd try doing both together, but always lost his balance, wobbling and sliding
to the ground. T. and I gazed entranced.

VII

SCOUTING FOR GIRLS

Making our own camp fires was my delight
at the bottom of the garden, propping twigs
into a little wigwam that would light
instantly when you struck a single match,
feeding it with bigger sticks until
it showed a fierce red heart and radiant embers,
just as *Scouting for Boys* by Baden-Powell
(I longed to be a Scout) recommended.

Gripping the long steel forks that Daddy gave us
one for each, we ate smoky toast
dry, or speared the baked potatoes
we'd covered up with burning sticks to roast.
Then we'd dribble water over the hot
red embers, making them hiss and turn black.

VIII

READING

Once I had ploughed through all the *Beacon Readers*
I graduated to 'The Cat That Walked'
and ate up everything the Woman cooked
from roasted marrow-bones to coriander,
walked on my wild lone through the Wet Wild Woods
and tricked her into giving me the warm
white milk I wanted.
                 Hunting for more food
I browsed my parents' shelves until I came
on Malory's *Morte D'Arthur* and fell in love
with every joust of helmed and armoured knights.
Their endlessly repeated wounds and fights
and Launcelot sent mad by Guinevere's
unkindness, running naked in sharp showers,
were so delicious I couldn't get enough.

IX

FRIENDS (i)

Two kinds of friendship even in babes,
Two against one and Seven against Thebes.
– W. H. Auden

T. and I were each other's best companion,
playing Let's Pretend games with our dolls,
'This is Teddy. This is the Chief Mourner',
telling stories in bed of Teddy Tail's
Africa, where Teddy and his friend
speared their enemies. We passed Cat over –
we didn't want the baby in our games.
Mummy saying we were like the Ugly Sisters
didn't make us nicer.

                                At school I played
with Bonnie, an American with brown
skin I admired and curling dark hair. When
she left, my new friend David helped me lay
imaginary fires and took me where
his father sharpened tools in silver showers.

X

DOWNING COLLEGE NATURAL HISTORY MUSEUM

I didn't care much for the axolotls,
primitive salamanders which like newts
develop from gilled larvae into adults
but often don't mature to adult shape,
some never getting past their tadpole stage
(Daddy's pet parable for use in schools).
The dozing python curled inside its cage
was duller than its name, electric eels
could neither shock nor thrill behind their glass,

unlike the ranks of horned or antlered skulls
and white articulated skeleton
looming over us, of the giant Bone
Elephant with his curving ivory tusks
rigid as Aaron's serpent, smooth and still.

XI

EASTER GARDENS

On Easter Eve Mummy took us three
looking for flowers to make the Easter garden,
driving off to search on Royston Heath
the grey-green waste of grass in which lay hidden
the purple Pasque Flower with its silky leaves,
then on to Hardwick Wood for violets,
primroses and budding twigs for trees.
Back home we picked small mauve primulas
and blue grape hyacinths, not too tall
for us to stick in wet moss.
                              Last, from our gravel
path we took stones to build a little cell
closed by a larger flint Mummy would move
that night, putting inside a piece of fabric
to be Christ's white shroud folded in the tomb.

XII

WINTER EVENING

I sat one evening at the kitchen table
Mummy once bought for five bob
at an auction, deep in an adult novel,
Kingfishers Catch Fire by Rumer Godden,
reading how the mother takes Teresa
her timid child, to settle in Kashmir,
blind to risk, deaf to her daughter's pleas
sending her out to hostile villagers
who stone the child and leave her there for dead.

How could this be? For there T. sat unharmed,
sewing her doll's dress by our kitchen stove,
chatting away to Mummy as she darned
jerseys and socks. Watching them both,
I shut the book I wished I'd never read.

The bone elephant said,
"Oh don't you dread,

The men
And that hen
That spoil the chameleans
wredding,
But at least they do bring
bedding.
That hen did make
A jolly good cake,
And the man made some
bedding and a ring
And a clock that went
ping ring ring!
The head of a deer
Said isn't it green
That the snake
Should rake
With her tail
Of mail.
The whale
Said "I hope it does not
fail,
At the marriage
Or they will have to drive
there in a carriage.

XIII

WRITING

I wrote in red with my first fountain pen
The people are asleep, the calm black shadows
from their places peep, fast as words came
into my head, *Now sits alone the widow,*
happily scrawling page after page of rhymes
for Daddy's birthday book (I have it still),
never guessing that in a little while
at the Perse School, I'd find it all come real.

Those calm black shadows will be here to stay
when I'm sitting at a desk alone
thinking of Latin and Greek irregular verbs,
half-hearing chatter and giggles I won't share,
watching the groups I won't be asked to join,
learning how to feed loneliness on words.

XIV

1, SPRINGFIELD, SIDGWICK AVENUE

Our walnut tree grew among crocus, scillas,
celandines and snowdrops on a lawn
bordered by daffodils. A shaggy tall
yew hedge marked the border of Finella
with its unfriendly children and bore in season
bright red poison-berries.
                              Our rooms were high
and dark, 'carefully planned to keep out light'
said Mummy, and in winter barely heated
by an underground coal-burning boiler. T.
and I were meant to help stoke this, taking
red-hot clinkers out with tongs to cool,
a chore we always tried to dodge. I
did better with the outdoors job of raking
green-gold leaves off the lawn in the autumn chill.

XV

AUTUMN TERM 1957

'Absences, 36' – the Junior Perse
registered us twice daily so that report
doubles them; even so, a quarter
of that first term was taken up by illness.
Mumps saved me from Miss Wilson's rage when I
was caught scratching my name on my desk lid
with my compass. Stabbing pain and high
fever took me to the children's ward

in Addenbrooke's for hours and hours of thirst,
being told off because I wouldn't eat
lumpy mince or use the pot, and worst
of all a post-operative enema,
soapy water, rubber tubing, shame
of bringing out big lumpy coils of shit.

XVI

COLOURED INKS

Appendicitis brought me time off school
to convalesce and better still, a set
of artists' coloured inks, black, crimson, blue,
purple and emerald, in jewel-bright
'Kandahar' bottles, together with a fine
tipped sable brush, even some golden ink –
all get-well presents from kind Uncle Van
my Dutch godfather, really called Jonkheer
Frederick van Kretschmar.
                                        I lay and planned
how all my Christmas cards that year would glow
like stained glass windows: a deep blue sky, a gold
star over a dark stable; amber sands
crossed by my Kings in striped and spotted robes,
purple and orange, Prussian blue and rose.

XVII

THE RIVER

Snobbs' Bathing Sheds, only ten minutes ride
by bike across Coe Fen, had a pond
for learners – murky water over mud
slimy enough under your toes to prompt
quick learning. Once you'd swum its twenty yards
you were allowed in the real Cam to float
under the willows by the bank or splash
across the river's width.
                              Nearer home
was Newnham Millpond where I tried to fish
without result, except once when a gudgeon,
was given me by a fisherman to take home
to cook and eat. It tasted like fried mud.
My own line wouldn't reach beyond the shallows
and sunlit brown-gold ooze of the pool's brim
brushed by darts of disappearing minnows.

Chapter I

In the beginning was the Word, and the Word was with God, and the Word was God.

The same was in the beginning with God.

All things were made by Him; and without Him was not any thing made that

XVIII

ILLUMINATIONS

Drawing my own illuminated *A*
for History homework led me to the Fitz-
william museum's parchment manuscript
Liber Horae, unreadable by me.
Gazing through burnished pillars of an *H*
at tiny men bent low to cut their corn
or through the arch of *O* at a green lawn
dotted with flowers, I planned to illustrate
with my own inks the gospel of St John.

In the Beginning was a golden *I*
branching in flowers. Trees and a laden vine
a three-tailed goat, a parrot, a honey-bee,
a blue and purple horse danced in a garden
of pleasure round my half-completed margin.

XIX

THE WILDERNESS

Up Sidgwick Avenue doors and brick walls hid
a wilderness of shaggy yews tangled
in purple nightshade, bryony and brambles
high dead grass, thistles and golden-rod
dark resinous cedars that were home
to finches, wrens and tiny goldcrests, bright
poppies, red, pink, violet streaked with white
in deep red oat-grass, all due to become
the Faculty of History's building site.

Heaps of excavated subsoil frowned
at themselves reflected in opaque
yellow spreading pools where Cat and I
played explorers scrambling up the brown
crumbling cliffs to find St Helena's Bay.

XX

DOCTOR FAUSTUS (i)
PUPPET PLAY

Having first made the head from plasticine,
you covered it with home-made papier-mâché,
split that when dry, glued it and painted on
eyes and mouth. You sewed the dress, attaching
the neck (your glove). And then you wrote your play.
Now that the gloomy shadow of the earth
leaps from the Antarctic world into the sky
and dims the welkin with her pitchy breath,
Faustus, begin thine incantations
summoning devils to obey his will.

I stitched my puppet's head onto a velvet
dress like a priest robed in purple for Advent,
humming the hymn *O Come, Emmanuel,*
practising invocation for the classroom.

XXI

DOCTOR FAUSTUS (ii)
INVOCATION

Very soon I wished I'd never begun
on Faustus and his spells. My puppets failed
to interest, let alone entertain
my classmates. I became the child
too clever to fit in, who never had
a partner when we walked in crocodile.

During one of my empty dinner-hours,
I traced a pentagram's outline in the cool
playground dust, whispering the devil's name.
At once I saw a darkness in my thought
take demon-shape: *You called me. I have come.*
What will you do? I couldn't answer that.
Knowing the action wouldn't make him go,
I brushed my sign out with a furtive shoe.

XXII

DOCTOR FAUSTUS (iii)
SPELL

In daytime darkness I rejoined my class,
walked in the crocodile to afternoon
lessons as usual in the Junior House,
sat at my desk alone and not alone
in darkness doing the French exercise
Miss Wilson set, hearing all the time
the whispering voice of Mephistophilis
What will you do? I'd called him, he had come
to fill my mind with darkness.
                             I went home
to English prep, potato cheese, then bed
in terror. I couldn't speak to Mum.
After two more haunted days, I did.
The Latin prayer she gave me, *Libera me,*
returned me to the normal light of day.

XXIII

PRIZE BOOK

At the end of term I won my first Form Prize
and hung round Heffer's bookshop wanting to find
a clothbound book to take the school's crest, priced
not more than ten shillings. What I longed
for most was coloured pictures like the book
given me by my godfather of Botticelli
paintings and drawings, but even as paperbacks
which weren't allowed, art books cost too much.

And then I found it: *Edible and Poisonous
Fungi* at eight and six, with colour plates:
Boletus edulis the Cep, 'warm brown
with paler edges, like a penny bun'
and horrible fascinating *Amanita
phalloides*, sickly greenish-white Death Caps.

XXIV

BLOOD ON THE DINING ROOM FLOOR

The evening of the day I got my award
and took it home, my sister Cat and I
fought. She wanted me to play
and all I wanted was to read about
how you laid out fungus caps to get
the spore-print of the slimy azure blue
Verdigris Agaric. 'Why can't you
stop bothering me?'

      Half joking, Cat pulled out
a grapefruit knife from the open drawer
and swiped me with it. We were taken aback
to see my blouse turn red. 'You idiot!
Look what you've done!' Mummy was appalled.
I got three stitches in my arm but not
a single bloodstain on my fungus book.

XXV

WEEKLY ROUTINES

Fridays were special – creamy scrambled eggs,
grilled kippers sometimes, or Mummy might make
on the best mornings, her buttery rich
kedgeree, toast and bitter marmalade
before the crowded lonely day of school.
Fried fish for supper, then two blessed days'
family freedom from my school-time role
of solitary outsider. Saturdays
meant fruit-and-veg shopping in Cambridge market
or standing in the bacon queue at Sainsbury's.
Gentleman's Relish mostly took my pocket
money, and the Public Library
my afternoons. Roast beef and Daddy home
lit Sundays up before the coming gloom.

XXVI

THE BURBAGE STORIES

Weekdays in term we barely saw our father
except at breakfast, and not always then
if after chapel he'd invited freshmen
to eggs and bacon in his college room.
But every mealtime of the holidays
we begged for an instalment of his serial
adventures of the Burbage family,

how the son tied a kite-string to the handle
of a pram during a gale, then won a prize
pig in a raffle, and how their *au pair,*
engaged to an undergraduate at Caius
College, dallied with a man at Clare
and the two students duelled as it had been
wild boars in the Burbage drawing room.

XXVII

FRIENDS (ii)

A lasting pleasure was to get letters from
Father Gilby the Dominican and (I learned
later) Aquinas scholar, whose crabbed hand
in black italic inscribing my own name
greeted me with fantasy and jokes,
rhymes, riddles and gallantries: *Accept,*
Mademoiselle, my sentiments of deep respect
and high devotion. I sent him drawings
and got an ode back on baptismal names:
Anceſtral poſtmen to the Habſburg Crown
Will gather round the font and, ghoſtly, frown
if *Thurn und Taxis* (what was that?) were shamed
as *Ernst* or *Adolf.* All his letters have
the parting benediction *Blessings and love.*

XXVIII

SUMMER IN WALES

Day after sunlit day the Irfon's stream
fed by peat bogs, ran transparent brown
'like bathing in sun-warmed silk', said Mum.
Teresa helped Cat teach herself to swim
(I'd learned that in the Cam) in waist-deep pools
where all our skins looked golden under water
as if we were a fairy-tale king's daughters,
holding her as she splashed and kicked the cool
shallows.
      And then our house spring ran so low
we had to trudge with heavy buckets
up from the riverside to flush the toilet
or, which was easier, from down the road.
The Hopes had plenty and would let us take
pails and pails of water, cold and sweet.

XXIX

PRESERVING FRUIT

In autumn when our garden trees were thick
with ripening fruit and nuts, grey squirrels got
most of the walnut crop unless we picked
green nuts which Mum would put away in salt
and vinegar, which turned them black and juicy,
better than olives for her daubes and pizzas.
Scarlet crab and yellow quince were turned
to clear red jelly and crimson-brown quince cheese, a
treat with cream. Trees that were silver-white
in spring were loaded now with fruit, some hard
and only fit for chutney, others sweet
for spicy pears, till all her shelves were full
of candied apple, quince and plum and gourd
she'd boiled and stirred while we three were at school.

XXX

ENGLISH LITERATURE

Lessons in English Literature were pure
enjoyment – lovely Christabel undressed,
Madeline in her charmed sleep, Wordsworth's hare
racing in joy to raise a sparkling mist
from the moorland where the leech-gatherer
met by a pond, entered the poet's dream,
the shining water-snakes that coiled and swam
in fiery tracks under a rising moon
nothing could dim, not even Miss Harrison's
weekly assignations of such tasks
as 'Paraphrase the following twenty lines
of *Hamlet*', or 'Analyse the part
played by' some character, Angel Clare in *Tess*,
the Fool in *Lear* – it couldn't matter less.

XXXI

WHITE ON BLACK, BLACK ON WHITE

On the matt surface of the scraper board
as featureless and black as ancient night
my cutting tool outlines a twisted shape,
bent trunk, branches, bare twigs – maybe dead,
more likely stripped by cold. At the top
one solitary leaf's dancing, its veins
white in the chill stare of a gibbous moon
(we've just read 'Christabel' in class), crossed
by one snaky bough.
                    Mummy doesn't care
for this, she likes my elephant adorned
with stripes and spirals being welcomed in
by crowds in black on white. But I prefer
the secret black and midnight thing I've drawn,
my twisted winter tree and glaring moon.

XXXII

WINTER MORNING 1962

Each willow tree along the Cam
stood stiff and prickly with white spikes.
River-mists blanked out the morning sun,
freezing inch-long daggers on the twigs
jagged as trees I'd drawn in Indian ink
or scratched in white on black scraper board
with twisted limbs and bent distorted trunks,
solitary outliers of the Wild Wood.

Sunshine covered the willows with bright drops
like King Frost rewarding the brave girl
who didn't wriggle in his icy grasp,
crowning her with diamonds and pearls
for three times answering his *Are
you warm, little girl?* with a polite *Yes, Sir.*

XXXIII

WINTER AFTERNOON

That was the great cold when the river froze
for three whole months, and all of us went skating,
the only winter we were warm at home
having for once turned on our central heating.
T. decided to lash out five pounds
on real Fen runners, but we others wobbled
taking turns to use Granny Mont's
skates that had lost half their lace-up bobbles.

When T. and I skated to Grantchester
we saw in the scratched ice, six inches deep,
a fish motionless as a fly in amber
beneath us as we slid past willow trees
black against sunset staining rosy colour
on snowy fields and rigid broken reeds.

XXXIV

KING'S COLLEGE CHAPEL

The door opened on dusky height, unseen
since they cleaned up the red and violet shafts
of light struggling through murky glass
to colour stone greyhounds and unicorns.
When sunshine brightened the Nativity,
sooty heaven and red-gold coats of arms
in the windows, you could barely see
the lofty vaulted ceiling through the gloom
thickened by centuries of candlelight.

Lighten our darkness: flames in choir and nave
blackened the stone and glass with sacred dirt
and lit the chorister whose treble led
the carol service every Christmas Eve,
singing sweetly of the cattle shed.

XXXV

THREE SISTERS: HEADS (i)

T. was sixteen, I fourteen and Cat ten
when Mum inherited a legacy
and used it to commission Betty Rea
to sculpt our heads. First Teresa, then
Cat and I took the bus for Papermills
outside Cambridge. Betty lived near green
grass and the grey stone Leper Chapel we
knew from Sunday School.
                          Acker Bilk's
'Stranger on the Shore' played as we sat
to Betty. I watched her build Cat's rounded face
and my forehead and brows from the red clay
she gave us to make our own models that
she fired in her own kiln. Until the end
of those sittings, Cat and I were friends.

XXXVI

THREE SISTERS: HEADS (ii)

Our three finished heads with their clear contours
of chin and throat were fired and cast in grey
fibreglass cement. Teresa's face
looks the most grown-up and serious.
I, not quite a child, am gazing at
invisible horizons. Long thick hair,
wide smile and rounded cheeks make Cat appear
the bonniest of us all.

                       Betty put
our heads into her show with a small figure
of a mother with her child reaching out
which Mum liked. I wanted to buy the naked infant
in bronze, no cherub but a new-born boy
life-size and yawning, animal yet human
legs still bent as if inside the womb.

XXXVII

HOLIDAY HOUSE (i)
CELLAR

Our parents made a chapel in the cellar
which had been our play-room on wet days
when stone steps leading down to darkness made
an entrance to a gaol or haunted chamber.
And then its stone shelf, furnished with a cross,
became the altar where my surpliced father
conducted those appalling services
for myself, Teresa and our mother
(Cat was too young) *kneeling upon our knees.*

His swinging stole reflected candle-flames
on the altar lighting up the plea
written in smoke above us *Help me, I*
have been a prisoner for 40 years
flickering and indelible as a dream.

XXXVIII

HOLIDAY HOUSE (ii)
BATHROOM

The bathroom was a lean-to off the kitchen,
lined with tongue-and-groove painted brown planks
and a deep bath, longer than at home.
Water came much hotter, spluttering
straight from the boiler, coloured brown by peat
but soft, so that soap would lather easily.

No electricity, you lit a candle
if you wanted any light to read.
In the daytime nettles and apple boughs
filled the high casement with green leaves and light.
When you were done you went to get your towel
warmed by the Rayburn, wiping off the grit
and coal-dust from the flagstones where you'd splodged
dark grey prints that faded as you watched.

XXXIX

MINIATURE HOUSE

Four matchboxes made a house for dolls.
The white-walled kitchen had a frieze of spring
onions and radishes, Rayburn and table with
red apples on a tiny cockle shell
as dish. The bedroom had a narrow couch
and wooden dressing-table half an inch high
whose bead-handled drawers could hold inside
bright paper dresses, below a framed pine-tree
in silhouette, with moon. A small shell made
a basin, and a bigger one the bath
for the adjoining bathroom. Balsa wood
bookshelves lined the cosy sitting room
where blue-green cushions on a velvet rug
waited forever for guests who never came.

XL

CLOUD-CUCKOO-LAND

When Miss Genochio produced *The Birds*
played by her own pupils in ancient Greek
I went with my parents to watch Teresa
cast as the Cuckoo. I didn't get the words
except 'Kokkoo' but liked the chorus song
set to the tune of 'Bye Bye, Blackbird.' Three
years later she took the players and me
up to London to see Karolos Koun's
Aldwych Theatre production in Modern Greek,
Cloud-Cuckoo-Land defying the regime
of army colonels.
                    I loved the colour, lightness,
whirling dances and jazzy Theodorakis
numbers. Miss G. observed the flightiness
half admiringly. 'It's very free.'

XLI

A WINTER'S TALE

Exit pursued by a bear, red-mouthed and roaring
hungrily while a rumbling thunderstorm
threatens. *I never saw the heavens so dim
by day* – my cue to shamble onstage, clawing
Antigonus who's just laid down the babe
Perdita on a grim deserted shore
prowled by beasts like me, who must ignore
the wailing easy meat so as to grab
 the courtier whom I'll tear apart and gorge
offstage.
         Rehearsing this in the school hall
one autumn evening under shadowy boards
inscribed with names of prize-winners, we heard
*President Kennedy's been shot in Dallas
Texas,* spreading silence like a wave.

XLII

OUTSIDER SCHOOLDAYS

Dinner breaks meant long hours of reading
in *Les Miserables* about the nest
a feral boy makes high up in a decaying
life-size fake elephant to be safe from rats
and once shares with the hero. Apart from needling
by one girl with her compass, no one spoke
or looked my way, unless occasionally
someone was stuck and needed help from me
untangling her Latin.
               During Greek
lessons in the Biology Lab, Miss Coke
teaching irregular verbs *tête-à-tête,*
turned my shoulders gooseflesh when her arm
encircled me. I glowered and sat tight
flinging back the cold correct response
'*Ago*, I lead. *Amuno,* I defend.'

XLIII

DEAD LANGUAGES

Dual Persons, Subjunctives, Optatives
for wishing others dead, the Middle Voice –
("I do this for myself") offered a way
of traversing grammar's complexities,
plaiting words in and out to make a web
of threaded sentences whose knots and loops
could capture unknown meaning from the books
and let me into philosophic depths.

But all I found in thought was poisonous
guilty hatred of the classmates who
didn't want me. In my dead languages
I lurked in an unwanted solitude
furiously pulling up an empty sieve
from a dark stream where nothing good could live.

XLIV

DARK THOUGHTS

I did the work for O-levels inside
an unseen prison cell like Bunyan's man
whose despair has locked him in an iron
cage. Or like *The Bell Jar*, although then
all I knew of Plath was 'Little Fugue,'
the black yew waving at an eyeless sky
Donald Davie had spoken of at school,
cold white clouds deaf to the poet's cry
I am guilty of nothing.

                     I couldn't speak about
this to my parents, or to anyone.
In the Latin exam, having finished long
before the others, I sat writing down
dark thoughts on the scrap paper which would not
unlike my answers, be read by anyone.

XLV

ADVANCED CLASSICS (i)
TRANSLATION

The formulaic words of the *Iliad*,
the *rosy-fingered dawn,* the *wine-dark sea*
spoke of fury, grief and distant gods
watching men's battles from a high blue sky
promising nothing. Catullus' voice demanding
thousands of kisses *before perpetual night*
takes us or angry and betrayed, attracted
us more than learning Horace odes by heart.

Yet we had pleasure when we tried to frame
our own metrical versions. *See how the boughs*
crack with their weight of snow, and how the streams
crystallize into sharp and stabbing ice
making the wine glow redder in its glass,
tuning a bright girl's *pleasing traitor laugh.*

XLVI

ADVANCED ENGLISH LITERATURE

Reading *I wake to feel the fell of dark*
gave me a sensation of relief.
Someone else had known it, that was enough.
Chaucer's *poudrés* and *alembikés eke*
were fun to learn by heart. Otherwise
A-level English Lit was pretty dull.
'What do the Marabar Caves symbolize?'
'Describe the character and dramatic role
of Cleopatra.'
     Yet I found new plays
to watch, coffee to share, 'Penny Lane'
and 'Strawberry Fields' on Radio Caroline.
In *Spring Awakening* all young people came
to sad ends, but we wouldn't, that was then.
Now was the Sixties, the future would be fine.

XLVII

CAT'S SONNET FOR MISS HARRISON

'The leaves float on the wind like coins of gold
And fall into the water, shining black
As ebon coffin.'
                'Only coins can't float.
Isn't she going to blue-pencil that?'
'She won't. *Love dies, flowers perish, colour fades,*
Liz Taylor too must sink beneath the grass
And martyrs, saints and eke prophetic maids.'
'Maids? What d'you mean?'
                  'Look at Joan of Arc
and in the Bible, the prophetic daughters
in the house of Philip of Caesarea.'
'Much too far-fetched!'
                 'No, the ending ought to
carry that, if I make it sound sincere.
How about *All beauty ends in tears*?'
Later: 'Well, did she twig the hoax?'
'She loves my sonnet. She's giving me top marks!'

XLVIII

CARPENTRY

Because the Ladies' evening class was full
I was allowed to join the Men's to learn
from a grey patient teacher how to rule
and chisel a slot just one inch deep by one
and five-eighth inches, then to saw the tongue
that fitted, then to shave wood till its grain
lay sheer and clear as poetry. Before long,
he said 'You know enough to make a plain
small table.'
             'What shall I use ?'
                            'Oak wood is best,
though it'll cost you.' So I set to work
on seasoned oak planks cut to size and dressed.
When after Christmas I was ordered back
to the Ladies, I carried on among
nailed-up gimcrack, making my table strong.

XLIX

ADVANCED CLASSICS (ii)
GREEK PROSE WITH MISS GENOCHIO

Translating out of English into Greek
meant I should render in their proper styles
passages from the English classics like
The harvest moon wades deep in cloud and hail.
She was displeased to find I couldn't cope
with *harvest moon*, which obviously implied
full moon (but what was *full?*), still less *wade deep*
which merely needed to be simplified
to *overshadowing clouds.*
                              But by now
too rattled even to think of *nephelé*
from *Nephelécoccygia* or *Cloud-*
Cuckoo-Land, feeling as dull as stone,
I had to leave the clouds and hail to her
trapped in the chill glare of that harvest moon.

L

SCHOLARSHIP CANDIDATE

Coleridge was the poet whom I chose
to work on for the Oxford Entrance paper,
using Mum's copy with her pencilled notes
which led me to his marvellous unknown river
running through caverns measureless to man,
like the Wolf's Leap where the Irfon river falls
into echoing darkness, caught and dammed
cunningly into pools and sinuous rills
in blossoming gardens.
                Leafing on, I fell
on words I read in fear and recognition,
the poet mourning that he could not feel
my shaping spirit of imagination
as he heard through the storm a lost child's wail
vanishing in the troubled sky's commotion.